COUNTRY PROFILE: IRAQ

COUNTRY

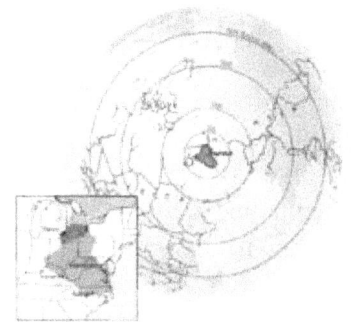

Click to Enlarge Image

Formal Name: Republic of Iraq (Al Jumhuriyah al Iraqiyah).

Short Form: Iraq.

Term for Citizen(s): Iraqi(s).

Capital: Baghdad.

Major Cities (in order of population size): Baghdad, Mosul (Al Mawsil), Basra (Al Basrah), Arbil (Irbil), Kirkuk, and Sulaymaniyah (As Sulaymaniyah).

Independence: October 3, 1932, from the British administration established under a 1920 League of Nations mandate.

Public Holidays: New Year's Day (January 1) and the overthrow of Saddam Hussein (April 9) are celebrated on fixed dates, although the latter has lacked public support since its declaration by the interim government in 2003. The following Muslim religious holidays occur on variable dates according to the Islamic lunar calendar, which is 11 days shorter than the Gregorian calendar: Eid al Adha (Feast of the Sacrifice), Islamic New Year, Ashoura (the Shia observance of the martyrdom of Hussein), Mouloud (the birth of Muhammad), Leilat al Meiraj (the ascension of Muhammad), and Eid al Fitr (the end of Ramadan).

Flag: The flag of Iraq consists of three equal horizontal bands of red (top), white, and black with three green, five-pointed stars centered in the white band. The phrase "Allahu Akbar" ("God Is Great") also appears in Arabic script in the white band with the word Allahu to the left of the center star and the word Akbar to the right of that star.

Click to Enlarge Image

HISTORICAL BACKGROUND

Early History: Contemporary Iraq occupies territory that historians regard as the site of the earliest civilizations of the Middle East. Because of its lush vegetation and ample water supply, ancient Mesopotamia (the land between the rivers, so named because the Oxus and Jaxartes rivers, now the Tigris and Euphrates, flowed through it) attracted settlers before 6000 B.C. In Sumer, or southern Mesopotamia, elements of early urban culture developed in response to the unpredictable natural rhythm of the rivers. The Sumerians introduced writing, literature, the wheel, astronomy, irrigation, and a highly developed sense of religion. Because the Sumerians worshiped the number 60, hours, minutes, and circles were divided into 60 units.

1

The Sumerians dominated southern Mesopotamia from 3360 B.C. until about 2000 B.C., when they were conquered by the Amorites. In the early eighteenth century B.C., the Babylonian king Hammurabi (whose dynasty took its name from the capital city of the Amorites, Babylon) established a complex law code upon which later civilizations based their laws. In the early sixteenth century B.C., the Hittite tribe destroyed Babylon and established a new kingdom, which collapsed around 1200 B.C. After a period of disunity, Mesopotamia was occupied by the Semitic Assyrians in the ninth century B.C. Hated for their cruel military rule, the Assyrians were overthrown by local tribes in 612 B.C. The Chaldeans, who succeeded the Assyrians, reestablished Babylon under King Nebuchadnezzar (ruled 605–562 B.C.). In 539 B.C., Cyrus the Great incorporated Mesopotamia into the Persian Empire. The conquest of Persian Babylon by Alexander the Great in the early 330s B.C. began a period of political disruption and brought substantial Greek influence into the region.

Iraq was conquered by the Parthians in 126 B.C. and by the Iranian Sassanians in 227 A.D. By 650 Arab tribes gained full control of the region from the Iranians, introducing Islam to what had been a mainly Christian group of tribes ruled by the Iranians in Iraq. The first great Arab dynasty, the Abbasid Caliphate, ruled the region from Baghdad between 750 and 1258. The fundamental schism of Islam, between the Shia and Sunni branches, which had occurred in the late 600s, stood in the background of the Abbasid and ensuing Islamic dynasties. A great Arab cultural flowering occurred under Al Mamun (ruled 813–33), but in the ninth and tenth centuries Turkish warriors, the Mamluks, achieved substantial influence under the Abbasids. The Mamluks' successors, the Seljuks, built a de facto empire around Baghdad before being conquered by the Mongols in the early thirteenth century. Under the leaders Chinggis Khan and, later, Timur, the Mongols destroyed much of urban Iraqi culture.

The Ottoman Period: Beginning in the early sixteenth century, the Sunni Turkish Ottoman Empire struggled against the Shia Persian Safavi Empire for control of Iraq. The Ottoman Empire controlled Iraq for most of the ensuing four centuries. However, the Safavis made substantial inroads, and Iraq was under the de facto authority of tribal confederations beginning in the seventeenth century. This trend was reversed in the eighteenth and early nineteenth centuries as the Mamluks took control of most of modern-day Iraq. After Mamluk rule ended in 1831, the *tanzimat* administrative and educational reforms of the Ottoman ruler Midhat Pasha increased the influence of urban culture in Iraq. In the same period, Western Europe established commercial outposts and brought technological advances to Iraq. Beginning in 1908, the influence of the pro-Western Young Turk faction in the Ottoman government introduced democratic concepts while alienating Arab parts of the empire by a campaign to centralize and "Turkify" Ottoman holdings.

By the early twentieth century, the decrepit Ottoman Empire was an area of conflict among the European powers. In World War I, British and Ottoman forces fought on Iraqi territory. After leading a revolt by Arab tribes in Iraq, Transjordan, and Syria, in 1917 the British occupied most of modern-day Iraq. Disappointing Arab ambitions for independence after the war, the Paris Peace Conference of 1919 made Iraq a British territory under a League of Nations mandate. The postwar British government faced nationalist sentiment that evolved into terrorist activity by secret societies. The Great Iraqi Revolution of 1920 united Shias and Sunnis and brought about an Arab provisional government headed by King Faisal, son of a Saudi royal line. Faisal never established legitimacy or stability in Iraq because he was not an Iraqi by birth; he remained under British control, and his government was predominantly Sunni.

Independent Iraq: Throughout the 1920s, nationalist Iraqis pressed the British for independence. Iraq became fully independent in 1932, retaining a special relationship with Britain. However, Iraq's formation into a state was hindered by the ongoing Shia–Sunni split, the ambitions of many factions to gain power in the new state, and the fragmenting effect of arbitrary borders and tribalism. Ethnic groups such as the Kurds and the Assyrians strongly resisted inclusion. In 1933 Assyrian resistance was marked by the massacre of several hundred Assyrian villagers by the Iraqi army. The death of Faisal in 1933 led to a successful coup against the destabilized government by General Bakr Sidqi, a Kurd, in 1936. In 1939 the death of Faisal's son Ghazi ended a period of Iraqi pan-Arabism and increased nationalism and anti-British sentiment. Subsequent decades would be marked by nationalism at home and quickly changing relations with Iraq's neighbors.

World War II brought new changes. In 1941 radical nationalist Rashid Ali overthrew the pro-British government of Nuri as Sad, precipitating a British invasion, restoration of the monarchy, and further alienation of the powerful nationalist factions from the Iraqi government. Beginning in 1943, Iraq was a base of Allied operations in the Middle East. The international stress of World War II exacerbated Iraq's economic and ethnic fragmentation and set the stage for two events of importance in 1948. An uprising, known as the "Wathbah," forced Iraq to renounce the Treaty of Portsmouth, which called for cooperation with Britain, and Iraq subsequently sent troops to fight in the first Arab-Israeli War. In the early 1950s, economic hardship increased sentiment against the government. Major protests occurred in 1952 and 1956. A new Arab secular party, the Baathists, grew from the intellectual community and gained support among the military. Inspired by Egypt's opposition to Iraq's membership in the British-led Baghdad Pact and by long-standing public unrest, in 1958 a revolt led by General Abdul Karim Qasim overthrew the monarchy and established a republic. Qasim's government failed to consolidate Iraq, however, and its overthrow by the Baath Party in 1963 began a period of coups, instability, and military domination in the mid-1960s. Following Iraq's controversial role in the Arab-Israeli War of 1967, the Baathists returned to power in 1968. In the ensuing decade, the Baath Party consolidated power under Ahmad Hasan al Bakr and Saddam Hussein. By 1970 the latter was the dominant force in Iraqi politics.

Iraq under Saddam Hussein: In the 1970s, Saddam Hussein was able to patch relations with most Arab states, substantially improve economic conditions, and in 1979 replace al Bakr as president of Iraq. Internally, he began a pattern of ruthless manipulation and extermination of enemies that would continue throughout his regime. In 1980 long-standing territorial disputes and the perception of Iran's weakness following its 1979 fundamentalist revolution led Iraq to invade Iran. Despite international mediation efforts, the ensuing war lasted until 1988 and killed between 500,000 and 1 million people. In the same period, Kurdish insurgents in northeastern Iraq took advantage of the war to press militarily and diplomatically for Kurdish autonomy. Iraq's invasion of neighboring Kuwait precipitated the Gulf War of early 1991 in which a United Nations (UN) force led by the United States defeated Iraq decisively. Withdrawal of that force from Iraq was followed by long-term arms restrictions, protected autonomous status for Iraq's

Kurds, and economic sanctions. Iraq's observance of arms restrictions became the subject of international controversy in the 1990s and early 2000s.

The 1990s were marked by new moves toward autonomy by the Kurds, periodic Iraqi resistance to arms inspections and "no-fly" restrictions in northern and southern Iraq, and progressive deterioration of living standards in Iraq because of international sanctions. A UN Oil-for-Food Program, established in 1997, did not relieve the domestic crisis. The terrorist attacks on the United States in 2001 brought a reassessment of U.S. policy toward Iraq as a threat to international stability. Although Iraq agreed to unconditional arms inspections in 2002, in March 2003 a coalition force led by the United States invaded Iraq on the grounds that the regime was concealing weapons of mass destruction and had supported the attacks of 2001. The invasion quickly toppled Saddam Hussein from power.

Post–Saddam Hussein: In mid-2003, the Coalition Provisional Authority established by the United States named an interim Coalition Governing Council of Iraqis, which was empowered only to facilitate the next stage of government formation. From 2003 through early 2005, insurgent and terrorist activities blocked the normalization of government and services, primarily in Sunni-dominated central Iraq. A provisional Iraqi government assumed nominal control in mid-2004, but U.S. and coalition forces remained in place without substantial reduction in 2006. In January 2005, a national election chose members of an interim parliament charged with electing an interim president and writing a constitution. Two months after a national referendum approved a new constitution in October 2005, a permanent parliament was elected. In June 2006, the approval of a full, permanent government under Prime Minister Nouri al Maliki followed months of harsh debate about power distribution among Iraq's major sects. The effectiveness of the new coalition government remained in doubt, however, and reconstruction of the economy and civil society remained slow. Meanwhile, the death of insurgent leader Abu Musab al Zarqawi in May 2006 was followed by an escalation of militia activity and terrorist attacks, especially on civilian targets close to Baghdad. In the early months of his administration, Maliki made sectarian reconciliation a top priority.

GEOGRAPHY

Location: Iraq is located in the Middle East at the northernmost extent of the Persian Gulf, north of Saudi Arabia, west of Iran, east of Syria, and south of Turkey.

Size: The total area of Iraq is 437,072 square kilometers, including 432,162 square kilometers of land surface.

Click to Enlarge Image

Land Boundaries: Iraq has common borders with the following countries: Iran, 1,458 kilometers; Jordan, 181 kilometers; Kuwait, 240 kilometers; Saudi Arabia, 814 kilometers; Syria, 605 kilometers; and Turkey, 352 kilometers.

Disputed Territory: Iraq's only border dispute, with Kuwait, was resolved by a United Nations commission in 1993. Both countries accepted the new demarcation.

Length of Coastline: Iraq's coastline totals 58 kilometers on the Persian Gulf.

Maritime Claims: Iraq claims 12 nautical miles of territorial sea and an unspecified distance of continental shelf.

Topography: Iraq has four main topographical regions. The desert zone of Iraq's west and southwest is part of the Syrian Desert, dominated by wide, flat, sandy expanses. The uplands region occupies most of Iraq's northern part, beginning about 120 kilometers north of Baghdad and including the watersheds of the Tigris and Euphrates rivers to the Syrian border. Although primarily desert, the region is characterized by deep river valleys. The third region is the northern highlands, which includes all of Iraq's northeasternmost territory and extends into neighboring Turkey and Iran. A series of elevation rises, interspersed with steppes, gives way to mountains as high as 4,000 meters near the Iranian and Turkish borders. The fourth region is the alluvial plain that extends from north of Baghdad southward to the Persian Gulf, following the lower Tigris and Euphrates rivers. The area, which is a large delta, includes lakes and marshlands. The extent of marshland in the alluvial plain varies according to the volume of water carried by the rivers in flood season. In their lower reaches, the two rivers break into several channels.

Principal Rivers: The Tigris and Euphrates, which rise in Turkey, form the dominant river system of Iraq. After flowing southward separately through Iraq for more than 2,500 kilometers, the rivers join about 150 kilometers north of the Persian Gulf to form the waterway known as the Shatt al Arab (literally, "Arab coast" because its southern extremity divides Arab Iraq from Persian Iran before flowing into the gulf). Several major tributaries of the Tigris flow through Iraq. The Khabur, the Great Zab, the Little Zab, the Uzaym, and the Diyala all flow into the Tigris from the northeastern highlands. The Euphrates has no tributaries in Iraq.

Climate: Most of Iraq has a desert climate with mild winters and dry, hot summers. The northeastern uplands have cold winters with occasionally heavy snowfalls. In the western desert and the northeastern foothills, average winter temperatures range from a low of 0° C to a high of 15° C, and average summer temperatures range from a low of 22° C to a high of 38° C. In the alluvial plain, the winter range is 4° C to 17° C, and the summer range is 29° C to 43° C. About 90 percent of Iraq's rainfall occurs between November and April. Except in the northern uplands and the northeastern highlands, average annual rainfall is 100 to 170 millimeters. In the uplands, the range is 320 to 570 millimeters, and in the mountains the annual total may reach 1,000 millimeters.

Natural Resources: Iraq's arable land has been rich and productive, particularly in the lower alluvial plain. The substantial amounts of arable land in the northwestern uplands region require irrigation. Because of its river systems, Iraq has the most abundant water reserves in its region. Hydrocarbons are Iraq's most important natural resource. Iraq has the third largest oil deposits in the world. Confirmed oil reserves total 112.5 billion barrels. Natural gas deposits are estimated at

3.1 trillion cubic meters, about 2 percent of total world reserves. Other mineral resources include phosphates, estimated to total 10 billion tons, and sulfur deposits located near Mosul.

Land Use: About 13 percent of Iraq's land surface is classified as arable; some 0.78 percent of the total land surface is planted to permanent crops. In 1998 some 35,250 square kilometers of cropland were irrigated.

Environmental Factors: Events of 1980–2006 have created environmental crises of emergency proportions. Military operations in three wars (1980–88, 1991, and 2003 to present) have left unexploded ordnance and land mines in exposed positions, killing or wounding an estimated 100,000 people in the early 2000s. Because of infrastructure damage, significant parts of the population do not have adequate water supply or sanitation systems, and sites where municipal and medical wastes have accumulated carry the risk of epidemic. The wartime destruction of military and industrial infrastructure has released heavy metals and other hazardous substances into the air, soil, and groundwater. Numerous spills have resulted from damage to Iraq's oil infrastructure, and the lack of water treatment facilities at Iraqi refineries has led to pollution from those installations. In the alluvial plain, soil quality has been damaged by the deposit of large amounts of salts, borne by irrigation overflows and wind and promoted by poor soil drainage. Desertification and erosion also have reduced arable land. Transboundary pollution and a lack of river basin management by the government have led to the degradation of Iraq's major waterways. Under Saddam Hussein, the government drained the extensive marshes in the lower reaches of the alluvial plain, changing water circulation and wildlife patterns over a wide area; beginning in 2004, some restoration has occurred. Flooding danger in the alluvial plain has decreased since construction of dams upstream on the Euphrates River. Although the interim government appointed in 2004 included a Ministry of Environment, long-term environmental crises such as the depletion of marshland in the Shatt al Arab have a low priority.

Time Zone: Iraq's single time zone is three hours ahead of Greenwich Mean Time.

SOCIETY

Population: In 2006 Iraq's population was estimated at 26,783,000, and the estimated growth rate was 2.7 percent per year. A general census was scheduled for late 2007. Average population density was 61.9 persons per square kilometer in 2006. The population occupies predominantly the alluvial plain and the northeast, leaving the western and southern desert regions very sparsely inhabited. The most densely populated governorate (province) is Baghdad, near the northern end of the alluvial plain, followed by Ninawa in the western section of the uplands region. Urbanization has been a strong demographic trend; between 1985 and 2005, the proportion of the population in urban areas increased from 69 percent to 79 percent. In the 1990s and early 2000s, an estimated 1 million Shias fled from southern Iraq to Iran to avoid persecution. Migration from Iraq to neighboring countries increased sharply with the overthrow of Saddam Hussein in 2003. In 2005 as an estimated 650,000 Iraqi refugees moved to Jordan and Syria; the latter received the great majority of the refugees, as it had since 2003. In 2006 the government estimated that 100,000 Iraqis had been internally displaced by sectarian violence.

Demography: In 2006 an estimated 39.7 percent of the population was 14 years of age or younger, and an estimated 3 percent was 65 years of age or older. Slightly more than 49 percent of the population was female. The birthrate was 32 births per 1,000 population, and the death rate was 5.4 per 1,000 population. The infant mortality rate was 48.6 per 1,000 live births. Life expectancy was 67.8 years for men and 70.3 years for women. The fertility rate was 4.2 births per woman.

Ethnic Groups: In 2006 an estimated 75 to 80 percent of the population was Arab and 15 to 20 percent, Kurdish. Other significant minority groups, together constituting less than 5 percent of the population, were Assyrians, Chaldeans, and Turkmens.

Languages: According to the constitution of 2005, the two official languages of Iraq are Arabic and Kurdish, which is official in regions with a Kurdish majority. Turkmen and Assyrian neo-Aramaic also are official languages in regions where they are spoken. The two main regional dialects of Arabic spoken in Iraq are Mesopotamian (spoken by about 11.5 million) and North Mesopotamian (spoken by about 5.4 million). Other languages in Iraq are Armenian, Azeri, and Chaldean neo-Aramaic.

Religion: The constitution of 2005 guarantees freedom of religion but specifies that no law may be enacted that is contrary to the teachings of Islam, the state religion. Some 97 percent of Iraq's population is Muslim. Of that number, 60 to 65 percent is Shia and 32 to 37 percent Sunni. Although the Shias have constituted more than half of Iraq's population throughout the twentieth century, until 2005 all governments excluded them from proportional political power. The Sunni regime of Saddam Hussein systematically repressed the Shias. In 1991 a Shia revolt in southern Iraq brought mass executions and further alienation, and in the post-Hussein era, the Shia–Sunni split remains a key political factor. The Kurds are predominantly Sunni but ethnically different from the Arab Sunnis and of a less militant religious orientation.

In 2003 an estimated 700,000 to 900,000 Christians were in Iraq, mostly belonging to the Eastern-rite Chaldean Catholic Church. However, between the late 1980s and 2004 an estimated 500,000 Christians left Iraq; in the post-Hussein era, the exodus accelerated because terrorists often attacked Christian targets. In late 2004, an estimated 40,000 Christians left after a series of bombings.

Education and Literacy: Following the regime change of 2003, the Coalition Provisional Authority, with substantial international assistance, undertook a complete reform of Iraq's education system. Among immediate goals were the removal of previously pervasive Baathist ideology from curricula and substantial increases in teacher salaries and training programs, which had been neglected in the 1990s. The new Ministry of Education appointed a national curriculum commission to revise curricula in all subject areas. Because of underfunding by the regime of Saddam Hussein, in 2003 an estimated 80 percent of Iraq's 15,000 school buildings needed rehabilitation and lacked basic sanitary facilities, and most schools lacked libraries and laboratories.

In the 1990s, school attendance decreased drastically as education funding was cut and economic conditions forced children into the workforce. After the regime change, the system included about 6 million students in kindergarten through twelfth grade and 300,000 teachers and administrators. Education is mandatory only through the sixth grade, after which a national examination determines the possibility of continuing into the upper grades. Although a vocational track is available to those who do not pass the exam, few students elect that option because of its poor quality. Boys and girls generally attend separate schools beginning with seventh grade. In 2006 obstacles to further reform were poor security conditions in many areas, a centralized system that lacked accountability for teachers and administrators, and the isolation in which the system had functioned for the previous 30 years. No private schools exist. Prior to the regime change of 2003, some 240,000 persons were enrolled in institutions of higher education. In 2003 the literacy rate was 56 percent for males and 24 percent for females.

Health: During its last decade, the regime of Saddam Hussein cut public health funding by 90 percent, contributing to a substantial deterioration in health care. During that period, maternal mortality increased nearly threefold, and the salaries of medical personnel decreased drastically. Medical facilities, which in 1980 were among the best in the Middle East, deteriorated. Conditions were especially serious in the south, where malnutrition and water-borne diseases became common in the 1990s. In 2005 the incidence of typhoid, cholera, malaria, and tuberculosis was higher in Iraq than in comparable countries. The conflict of 2003 destroyed an estimated 12 percent of hospitals and Iraq's two main public health laboratories. In 2004 some improvements occurred. Using substantial international funds, some 240 hospitals and 1,200 primary health centers were operating, shortages of some medical materials had been alleviated, the training of medical personnel had begun, and the inoculation of children was widespread. However, sanitary conditions in hospitals remained unsatisfactory, trained personnel and medications were in short supply, and health care remained largely unavailable in regions where violent insurgency continued. In 2005 there were 15 hospital beds, 6.3 doctors, and 11 nurses per 10,000 population. Plans called for US$1.5 billion of the national budget to be spent on health care in 2006.

In the late 1990s, Iraq's infant mortality rates more than doubled. Because treatment and diagnosis of cancer and diabetes decreased in the 1990s, complications and deaths resulting from those diseases increased drastically in the late 1990s and early 2000s. The collapse of sanitation infrastructure in 2003 led to an increased incidence of cholera, dysentery, and typhoid fever. Malnutrition and childhood diseases, which had increased significantly in the late 1990s, continued to spread. In 2006 some 73 percent of cases of human immunodeficiency virus (HIV)/acquired immune deficiency syndrome (AIDS) in Iraq originated with blood transfusions and 16 percent from sexual transmission. The AIDS Research Centre in Baghdad, where most cases have been diagnosed, provides free treatment, and testing is mandatory for foreigners entering Iraq. Between October 2005 and January 2006, some 26 new cases were identified, bringing the official total to 261 since 1986.

Welfare: Like the health system, Iraq's welfare system, one of the best in the Middle East in the 1980s, suffered drastic funding cuts in the 1990s as the regime shifted funds to other priorities. Beginning in the 1990s, damage to the economy by international sanctions dramatically reduced the standard of living and left a large portion of Iraqi society in poverty, despite the United Nations Oil-for-Food Program established in 1997. Average wages decreased drastically in the late 1990s. In the early 2000s, an estimated 60 percent of Iraqis were dependent on monthly food rations (for which all Iraqis were eligible beginning in 1990) from the Public Distribution System (PDS). In early 2005, that system and subsidized fuel distribution remained the main elements of the social safety net; nationwide shortages of sugar, milk, and ghee (a type of butter) were reported at that time. The PDS was inefficient and expensive, costing the government US$4 billion in 2005 because it continued to support all Iraqis regardless of income. In 2006 international donors sought to improve the targeting, and thus the cost-benefit ratio, of the PDS. According to an Iraqi labor expert, in 2005 more than 60 percent of the workforce was unemployed.

ECONOMY

Overview: Iraq's economy was badly damaged during the Iran–Iraq War (1980–88), and the international sanctions imposed following the Persian Gulf War of 1991 were another major blow. Aside from those events, reconstruction of a viable economy in the early 2000s encountered a severely distorted system. Under Saddam Hussein, the levers of economic power were solely in the hands of a corrupt elite in the ruling Baath Party; for the 25 years prior to 2003, no national budget was prepared. Under those circumstances, the private sector engaged mainly in illegal economic activity. Because Iraq's economy depends heavily on the oil industry, progress from the post-Hussein low point in 2004 depends on the rates at which that industry can be reconstructed and reintegrated into the world oil market. In 2006 economic development in Iraq depends first on improvement of the security situation, which greatly hindered economic progress in the first post-Hussein years. Most major enterprises remained in state hands when a permanent government took office in early 2006. Near-term government planning goals include budget deficit reduction, diversification of the economy through privatization, and reduction of unemployment. International grants and investments are an important source of funding for such goals. Privatization, which met strong resistance in the post-Hussein years, is to be accomplished in gradual stages. Government corruption is a serious obstacle to economic progress because it centers on agencies administering the oil industry. Iraq applied for membership in the World Trade Organization in 2004, but it had not been accepted as of mid-2006.

Gross Domestic Product (GDP): According to the World Bank, Iraq's GDP in the crisis year of 2003, US$12.1 billion, represented a drop of about 60 percent from the 2000 figure of US$31.8 billion. Because such a low point was reached in 2003, the figure for 2004, US$25.6 billion, amounted to an increase of 112 percent. The economy experienced a 3 percent decrease in productivity in 2005, yielding a GDP of US$24.3 billion, or US$907 per capita. In 2006 forecasts of future GDP growth varied widely because of the unpredictable revival pace of the oil industry. In 2004 industry contributed 66.6 percent of GDP, services 26.1 percent, and agriculture 7.3 percent.

Government Budget: The World Bank estimated that in 2003 government revenue was US$4.7 billion and government expenditures US$8.6 billion, resulting in a deficit of US$3.9 billion. The official 2004 budget of the interim government called for expenditures of US$33.5 billion and revenues of US$19 billion, incurring a deficit of US$14.5 billion. The 2005 budget included expenditures of US$24 billion and revenues of US$19.3 billion, a deficit of US$4.7 billion. The

Ministry of Finance's Budget Directorate was scheduled for reorganization and streamlining in 2006.

Inflation: In 2003 and the first half of 2004, estimates of inflation in Iraq ranged from 25 percent to 28 percent. Although inflation was under substantially tighter control by the end of 2004, in 2005 it again rose sharply to an estimated 40 percent.

Agriculture: Historically, only 50 to 60 percent of Iraq's arable land has been under cultivation. Because of ethnic politics, valuable farmland in Kurdish territory has not contributed to the national economy, and inconsistent agricultural policies under Saddam Hussein discouraged domestic market production. The United Nations Oil-for-Food Program (1997–2003) further reduced farm production by supplying artificially priced foreign foodstuffs. The military action of 2003 did little damage to Iraqi agriculture; because of favorable weather conditions, in that year grain production was 22 percent higher than in 2002. Although growth continued in 2004, experts predicted that Iraq will be an importer of agricultural products for the foreseeable future. The chief recipient of such imports is the Public Distribution System, which rations food to the population. Long-term plans call for investment in agricultural machinery and materials and more prolific crop varieties—improvements that the Hussein regime failed to make. In 2005 the main agricultural crops were wheat, barley, corn, rice, vegetables, dates, and cotton, and the main livestock outputs were cattle and sheep.

Forestry: Throughout the twentieth century, human exploitation, shifting agriculture, forest fires, and uncontrolled grazing denuded large areas of Iraq's natural forests, which in 2005 are almost exclusively confined to the northeastern highlands. Most of the trees found in that region are not suitable for lumbering. In 2003, 113,000 cubic meters of wood were harvested, nearly half used as fuel.

Fishing: Despite its many rivers, Iraq's fishing industry has remained relatively small and based largely on marine species in the Persian Gulf. In 2002 the catch was 14,500 tons.

Mining and Minerals: Aside from hydrocarbons, Iraq's mining industry has been confined to the extraction of relatively small amounts of phosphates (at Akashat), salt, and sulfur (near Mosul). Since a relatively productive period in the 1970s, the mining industry has been hampered by the Iran–Iraq War (1980–88), the international sanctions of the 1990s, and the economic collapse of 2003.

Industry and Manufacturing: Traditionally, Iraq's manufacturing activity has been closely connected to the oil industry. The major oil-related industries have been petroleum refining and the manufacture of chemicals and fertilizers. Before 2003, limitations on privatization and the effects of the international sanctions of the 1990s hindered the diversification of manufacturing. Since 2003, security problems have blocked efforts to establish new enterprises. An exception is the construction industry, which has profited from the need to rebuild after Iraq's several wars. In 2004–5 growth in construction was spurred by a government program to ease Iraq's serious housing shortage. In 2005 about 150,000 Iraqis were employed in short-term construction projects. That industry's main material requirement, cement, was the only major industrial product not based on hydrocarbons.

Energy: Possessing the third-greatest oil reserves in the world, Iraq has the resources for complete energy independence. By world standards, production costs for Iraqi oil are relatively low. However, long-term neglect and mismanagement of the petroleum industry by the Baathist regimes left the industry's infrastructure in poor condition. The lifting of international sanctions in 2003 allowed repairs to begin. However, since 2003 oil pipelines and installations have been sabotaged persistently, and in mid-2006 output had not regained pre-2003 levels.

In 2004 Iraq had eight oil refineries, the largest of which were at Baiji, Basra, and Daura. Sabotage and technical problems at the refineries forced Iraq to import fuels, liquid petroleum gas, and other refined products from nearby countries. In October 2004, for example, Iraq spent US$60 million for imported gasoline. In 2005 and 2006, regular sabotage of plants and pipelines reduced export and domestic distribution of oil, particularly to Baghdad. Nationwide fuel shortages and power outages resulted. In 2004 plans called for increased domestic utilization of natural gas to replace oil and for use in the petrochemicals industry. However, because most of Iraq's natural gas output is extracted together with oil, growth in gas output depends on developments in the oil industry. An expansion program in that industry for 2006 called for an expenditure of US$2 billion on new oil pipelines, storage facilities, export terminals, refineries, and wells, together with repair of damaged infrastructure, improved security, and streamlining of the delivery system. The plan would increase oil exports for 2006 to 568 million barrels, compared with the 2005 total of 508 million barrels. However, in 2006 the Ministry of Oil estimated that some US$25 billion was needed to repair damage and replace equipment.

As much as 90 percent of Iraq's power generating and distribution systems were destroyed in the Persian Gulf War of 1991, and full recovery never occurred. In 2006 Iraq had an estimated 5,000 megawatts of usable power-generating capacity, compared with 8,000 megawatts of demand. This discrepancy led to regular power outages, particularly in Baghdad, and to the importation of power from Iran and Syria. Although 98 percent of houses were connected to the power grid in 2005, for most customers electricity supply was extremely unreliable, and in 2006 factories received only 20 percent of the power needed to operate at full capacity. In 2005 plans called for the construction of several new power plants and restoration of existing plants and transmission lines to ease the blackouts and economic hardship caused by this shortfall, but sabotage and looting slowed expansion. In 2005 the World Bank estimated that US$12 billion would be needed for near-term restoration, and the Ministry of Electricity estimated that US$35 billion would be necessary to rebuild the system fully.

Services: Iraq's financial services have been the subject of reforms since the fall of Saddam Hussein. The 17 private banks established during the 1990s were limited to domestic transactions and attracted few private depositors. Those banks and two main state banks were badly damaged by the international embargo of the 1990s. To further privatize and expand the system, in 2003 the Coalition Provisional Authority removed restrictions on international bank transactions and freed the Central Bank of Iraq (CBI) from government control. In its first year of independent operation, the CBI received credit for limiting Iraq's inflation. In 2004 three foreign banks received licenses to conduct business in Iraq.

Because of the danger posed by Iraq's ongoing insurgency, the security industry has been a uniquely prosperous part of the services sector. Often run by former U.S. military personnel, in

2005 at least 60 companies offered personal and institutional protection, surveillance, and other forms of security. The companies employed an estimated 5,000 to 10,000 Iraqis and 8,000 to 15,000 foreign operatives and workers. In the early post-Hussein period, a freewheeling retail trade in all types of commodities straddled the line between legitimate and illegitimate commerce, taking advantage of the lack of income tax and import controls.

The Iraqi tourism industry, which in peaceful times profited from Iraq's many places of cultural interest (earning US$14 million in 2001), has been completely dormant since 2003. Despite these conditions, in 2005 the Iraqi Tourism Board maintained a staff of 2,500 and 14 regional offices.

Labor: In 2004 Iraq's labor force was estimated at 7.4 million people. Recent figures on labor participation by sector are not available. In 1996 some 66.4 percent of the labor force worked in services, 17.5 percent in industry, and 16.1 percent in agriculture. In 2005 estimates of Iraq's unemployment ranged from 30 percent to 60 percent. The actual figure is problematic because of high participation in black-market activities and poor security conditions in many populous areas. In central Iraq, security concerns discouraged the hiring of new workers and the resumption of regular work schedules. At the same time, in the early 2000s the return of Iraqis from other countries increased the number of job seekers. In 2005 most legitimate jobs were in the government, the army, the oil industry, and security-related enterprises. The overthrow of Saddam Hussein's greatly overstaffed government disrupted the input of large numbers of Iraqis to the economy. However, in 2005 the government of Ibrahim al Jafari made another cut in the public sector (which nonetheless still accounted for as many as half of Iraq's jobs), further reducing employment. In 2005 U.S. and Iraqi government authorities opened new training centers to alleviate unemployment, which threatened to augment the membership of insurgent groups. In early 2004, the official minimum wage was US$70 per month.

Foreign Economic Relations: From the 1990s until 2003, the international trade embargo restricted Iraq's export activity almost exclusively to oil. In 2003 oil accounted for about US$7.4 billion of Iraq's total US$7.6 billion of export value, and statistics for earlier years showed similar proportions. After the end of the trade embargo in 2003 expanded the range of exports, oil continued to occupy the dominant position. In 2004 Iraq's export income doubled (to US$17.8 billion), but oil still accounted for all but US$340 million (2 percent) of the total. In 2004 and 2005, sabotage significantly reduced oil output, limiting total export values. In 2004 the chief export markets (in order of value) were the United States (which accounted for 52 percent), Spain, Japan, Italy, and Canada. In 2004 the value of Iraq's imports was US$19.6 billion, incurring a trade deficit of about US$1.8 billion. In 2004 the main sources of Iraq's imports (in order of value) were Syria, Turkey, the United States, Jordan, and Germany. Because of Iraq's inactive manufacturing sector, the range of imports was quite large, including food, fuels, medicines, and manufactured goods.

Balance of Payments: The financial management and reporting system remained incomplete in 2005, making full evaluation of Iraq's financial situation problematic. In 2004 the World Bank estimated Iraq's current account balance at –US$3.8 billion after being in surplus for the previous three years. Information on the remaining elements of the balance of payments was not available.

External Debt: At the time it was deposed, the regime of Saddam Hussein had an estimated US$120 billion of external debt. In late 2004, the Paris Club of international creditors agreed to cancel 80 percent of the debt owed by Iraq to its 19 member nations, an amount estimated at US$42 billion. In 2005 a three-phase process was devised for this restructuring, which was to be conducted by the United Nations. The United States applied heavy pressure on creditor countries outside the Paris Club to take similar steps. The International Monetary Fund estimated Iraq's external debt for 2005 as US$68 billion (2.8 times gross domestic product—GDP) and forecast that the 2006 debt would be 2.2 times GDP.

Foreign Investment: Generally, in 2005 foreign investors awaited a quieting of insurgent activities before making large commitments. Although foreign banks received permission to do business in Iraq, security risks limited their activity. The Standard Chartered Bank of Great Britain, the multinational Hong Kong and Shanghai Banking Corporation (HSBC), and the National Bank of Kuwait received licenses to conduct banking transactions in Iraq, but a limit of six such banks was set until 2008. Iraq's Foreign Investment Law allows foreign banks to hold a 50 percent interest in Iraqi private banks. In 2005 the World Bank's International Finance Corporation joined the National Bank of Kuwait in buying a share of the Credit Bank of Iraq, a major infusion of money into the Iraqi financial system. In 2004 Shell, BP, and Exxon Mobil signed agreements to study Iraq's oil reserves, and an international consortium signed a small-scale oilfield development agreement with the Ministry of Oil. In 2006 Iraq set a goal of US$20 billion of foreign investment in its oil industry. In an effort to regularize procedures, in mid-2006 the Council of Ministers approved a new foreign investment law that met strong resistance in the Council of Representatives (lower house of parliament) because of its provisions for foreign ownership.

Foreign Aid: In the post-Saddam Hussein period, Iraq has received foreign aid from a number of national and international sources, but the United States has been by far the largest donor. For the period 2004–7, Iraq received pledges of US$33 billion in aid. In 2005 U.S. government aid to Iraq totaled US$10.2 billion, an increase from US$3 billion in 2004. For 2003–6 all forms of U.S. assistance totaled US$28.9 billion, 38 percent of which was designated for upgrading security and 40 percent for repairing critical infrastructure. In 2004 the U.S. Agency for International Development awarded contracts totaling US$900 million for capital construction, seaport renovation, personnel support, public education, public health, government administration, and airport management.

Among international contributors, the World Bank committed US$3 billion to US$5 billion for reconstruction over a five-year period, and smaller commitments came from Japan, the European Union, Britain, and Spain. Russia canceled 65 percent of Iraq's debt of US$8 billion, and Saudi Arabia offered an aid package totaling US$1 billion. Effective application of reconstruction funds depends on substantial improvement in infrastructural and institutional resources. Pending full resolution of Iraq's international debt situation, for the foreseeable future U.S. funds are expected to pay for capital investments in rebuilding. However, in 2004–6 security costs consumed an unexpectedly high percentage of aid allotments, to the detriment of reconstruction activity.

Currency and Exchange Rate: In October 2003, the new Iraqi dinar replaced the old Iraqi dinar as the official currency. In August 2006, its value, originally 1,950 to the U.S. dollar, had stabilized at 1,476 to the U.S. dollar.

Fiscal Year: Iraq's fiscal year is the calendar year.

TRANSPORTATION AND TELECOMMUNICATIONS

Overview: In the 1970s, a sustained campaign for economic development provided Iraq with elements of a high-grade ground transportation infrastructure. Further development of roads and railroads in eastern Iraq supported the war effort against Iran (1980–88). However, damage in the Persian Gulf War of 1991 was only superficially repaired, and the insurgent sabotage that began in 2003 brought another round of damage. Most of that damage was to be repaired by U.S. contractors and international aid organizations. Security conditions were a major factor determining the pace of such repairs. In 2004 the United States allotted US$500 million in aid for transportation upgrades.

Roads: In 2005 Iraq had about 39,000 kilometers of paved roads, many of which were broad highways constructed for military and commercial use in the 1970s and 1980s. Most road and bridge damage was repaired after the 1991 Persian Gulf War had targeted transportation infrastructure. However, beginning in 2003 main roads in central and northern Iraq, such as the connector between Baghdad and the Jordanian border, sustained repeated damage by saboteurs. Bridges damaged in 2003 by coalition forces were the focus of major repair operations in 2004.

Railroads: In 2005 Iraq had an estimated 2,400 kilometers of standard-gauge railroad track, connecting Baghdad with other Iraqi cities and foreign borders in several directions. In the early 2000s, only 30 percent of Iraq's commercial traffic moved by rail, in part because only 40 percent of locomotives were operable. Most of the railroad infrastructure was in poor repair; an estimated 70 percent of track was impassable at normal speeds, and improvements were very gradual in the early 2000s. Operations on the Baghdad–Mosul and Baghdad–Umm Qasr lines were restored following the government change of 2003, although service remained unreliable. Long-term plans call for new rail links with Syria and Iran.

Ports: In the later years of the Saddam Hussein regime, Iraq's ports suffered from poor maintenance and were littered with wreckage. In the post-Hussein years, three oil tanker terminals were operating in the Persian Gulf: Basra (the main oil port) and offshore terminals at Khawr al Amayah and Khawr az Zubayr (mainly for dry goods and natural gas). In October 2004, Basra's capacity was 2 million barrels of oil per day, and the planned capacity of Khawr al Amayah is 1.2 million barrels per day. Umm Qasr, which has benefited from major renovation since 2002, has 23 berths on the Shatt al Arab for general commercial use and delivery of emergency supplies.

Inland Waterways: Iraq has 5,275 kilometers of inland waterways, including canals and rivers that are considered major lines of communication. The main navigable waterways are the Euphrates River (2,815 kilometers) and the Tigris River (1,895 kilometers).

Civil Aviation and Airports: In 2005 Iraq had 78 airports with paved runways, including 20 with runways longer than 3,000 meters. Another 33 airports had unpaved runways. The three major international airports are at Baghdad, Basra, and Mosul. All major airports were damaged during the war in 2003, and since that time the coalition military force has been the major user. Restoration of the Baghdad and Basra airports was a high priority of the occupation force. In 2005 the Baghdad airport had an annual capacity of 7.5 million passengers. The national airline, Iraqi Airways, resumed a limited flight schedule to destinations in the Middle East in late 2004, but service was intermittent. In 2005 Athens and Istanbul were the only European destinations on its schedule. Regular connections began with Iran in 2005 and with Guangzhou, China, in April 2006. The European and Middle Eastern routes were expanded in early 2006, but high risks continue to limit the airline's routes and profits. After resuming service, Iraqi Airways was run by a Jordanian airline until the Iraqis severed the relationship in 2006, and the airline's financial backing has been unstable. A German air freight company is one of the few foreign lines serving Baghdad.

Pipelines: In 2005 Iraq had an estimated 5,418 kilometers of oil pipelines, 1,739 kilometers of natural gas pipelines, and 1,343 kilometers of pipelines for refined products. The system, which nominally is capable of transporting several million barrels of oil per day, has suffered severe damage in three military conflicts and in the sabotage that followed the 2003 war. The main oil export line is the 960-kilometer Kirkuk–Ceyhan dual line, which leads to the Black Sea and has a capacity of 1.6 million barrels per day. However, since 2003 the line has been either closed or operating at minimum capacity. A major line between Iraq and the Red Sea has a similar capacity but was confiscated by Saudi Arabia in 2001. The largest natural gas pipeline connects Baghdad with the West Qurnah field in southeastern Iraq.

Telecommunications: The war of 2003 severely disrupted telecommunications in all of Iraq. Since that time, the U.S. Agency for International Development has overseen repair operations by U.S. contractors, but sabotage has delayed restoration in some areas. In 2004 Iraq had an estimated 1 million conventional telephone lines, about half in the Baghdad area. Service was restored gradually to the large percentage of those lines that were not in service in 2003. As of 2005, some 25 conventional telephone exchanges and 14 satellite-linked switching stations were in operation, but international calling remained difficult. An insufficient technical infrastructure also has delayed the replacement of conventional telephone lines with fiber-optic lines. Construction of a mobile-phone system began in late 2003, and in 2005 an estimated 2.8 million mobile phones were in use. Three consortia received contracts to establish mobile phone service in the north, center, and south, respectively. In 2004–5 work in the northern region proceeded fastest, although the regional approach left gaps in service.

Internet access expanded rapidly after the war of 2003, following the end of full state control under the Saddam Hussein regime. In 2005 an estimated 36,000 people were using the Internet, and four hosts were in operation. In 2005 the main points of access were hotels and Internet cafés in Baghdad, Basra, and Kurdistan. Domestic Internet landlines remained unreliable.

GOVERNMENT AND POLITICS

Overview: In the years following the overthrow of Saddam Hussein, governance of Iraq passed through several stages. The Coalition Provisional Authority (CPA), established by the United States to govern the country immediately following the occupation, officially transferred sovereignty to an Interim Iraqi Government in June 2004. This was a first step in building a new, indigenous government structure in Iraq. The Transitional Administrative Law (TAL), functioning as an interim constitution until the end of 2005, called for Iraq to have a permanent republican, federal government system; power was to be shared among the central government, 18 governorates (provinces), and local and municipal governments. The autonomy of one region, Kurdistan, was specifically recognized. In January 2005, national elections to seat an interim parliament were a second step in establishing a permanent government. That parliament built the framework for the writing of a new constitution and the election of a permanent legislature.

After some delay, in October 2005 a two-thirds majority of voters ratified a new constitution, which had been created to replace the TAL by a 55-member panel representing the three main factions: Kurds, Shiites, and Sunnis. Although some elements remained in dispute, the new charter embodied the same fundamental elements as the TAL, describing Iraq as a "multiethnic, multi-religious, and multi-sect country."

In early 2006, a dispute among the factions over the post of prime minister delayed the formation of a permanent government. After the Shiite prime minister-designate, Ibrahim al Jafari, was unable to form a government, Nouri al Maliki, another leader of Jafari's party, was chosen to replace him in May 2006. A full permanent government, with ministries divided among the major factions, was in place in June, avoiding a major crisis but still facing bitter divisions among the populace.

Aside from an enormous economic restoration process, major issues face the first permanent government. They include improving its own tenuous legitimacy in the view of the country's factions, tightening porous borders, sharing oil revenues between the central government and the provinces (particularly those dominated by the Kurds), balancing strong central government with demands for regional sovereignty, and determining the role of Islamic law in government and jurisprudence.

Executive Branch: The constitution of 2005 calls for the executive branch to consist of a president and vice president; a prime minister; and a governing body, the Council of Ministers, that has an unspecified number of positions. The president has mainly ceremonial duties, and his decisions require the approval of the prime minister. The prime minister, who is selected by the president from the majority party of the parliament and with the parliament's approval, presides over the Council of Ministers, exercises executive responsibility for the running of the government, and acts as commander in chief of the armed forces. The Council of Ministers, whose members are nominated by the prime minister, is to plan and administer the general policies of the state, propose laws and budgets, negotiate treaties, and oversee the national security agencies.

In April 2005, the following individuals were chosen to lead the interim government through the approval of a constitution and election of permanent national officials: a Shia, Ibrahim al Jafari, as prime minister; a Kurd, Jalal Talabani, as president; and a Sunni, Hachim Hasani, as president of the National Assembly. Following approval of the constitution in October and parliamentary elections in December 2005, formation of a permanent government began. For a transitional period of one session of the legislature, executive power remained with a three-person Presidential Council consisting of the president and two vice presidents. The council's actions required unanimity among its three members. Talabani remained president; his vice presidents were the Shia Adil Abdul Mahdi and the Sunni Tariq al Hashimi. In the spring of 2006, Prime Minister Nouri al Maliki, who had replaced Jafari, was able to end months of political deadlock by gaining parliamentary approval of a full slate of 36 ministers, who constituted the first permanent government since 2003. Four ministers were women. In an attempt to broaden support for his government, in mid-2006 Maliki established the Supreme Committee for Reconciliation and National Dialogue, which included members from a wide cross-section of social groups.

Legislative Branch: The constitution of 2005 gives legislative power to two bodies, the Council of Representatives and the Council of Union. The Council of Union, whose form and role were yet to be determined in 2006, is to act as an appointive upper house representing the 18 governorates (provinces) of Iraq. The Council of Representatives, the working legislative body, consists of 275 members elected for four-year terms. The council is to pass laws; elect the president and generally oversee the executive branch; ratify treaties; and approve nominations of the prime minister, cabinet ministers, and other officials. The presidential election requires a two-thirds vote of the Council of Representatives; approval of the heads of ministries requires a simple majority.

The Council of Representatives convened for the first time under the new constitution in March 2006. Prior to that, in 2005 a unicameral, 275-member parliament, the National Assembly, had been elected as a transitional legislature to take the place of the 100-member Interim National Council, which the Coalition Provisional Authority had named in mid-2004. In the elections of January 2005 that chose the assembly, the Shia United Iraqi Alliance won 140 seats, the Democratic Patriotic Alliance of Kurdistan (a coalition of the two major Kurdish parties) won 75 seats, and a secular bloc, Iraqi National Accord, won 40 seats. Having largely boycotted the election, the substantial Sunni minority gained only 17 seats, but the Sunnis were allotted the position of speaker of parliament in a power-sharing compromise.

Upon ratification of the 2005 constitution, the parliament organized a new round of parliamentary elections leading to the formation of a permanent government. The elections of December 2005 revised somewhat the power balance among the major factions, adding substantially to Sunni representation. The United Iraqi Alliance won 128 seats (eight seats short of a majority), and the newly formed Sunni Iraqi Accord Front won 44. The Kurdish party won 53 seats, a loss of 22, and Iraqi National Accord won 25, a loss of 15. Mahmud Mashhadani, a Sunni, was elected president of the Council of Representatives in April 2006.

Judicial Branch: The constitution of 2005 calls for Iraq's judicial authority at the federal level to consist of the Supreme Federal Court and the Federal Court of Cassation (appeal). The

Supreme Federal Court is to rule on the constitutionality of laws, on conflicts between federal and sub-federal authorities, and on cases involving federal law. The constitution calls for the court to include experts on Islamic law, but the composition and appointment authority of the court are left to legislation. Appointments to the Supreme Federal Court and the Federal Court of Cassation are made by recommendation of the Supreme Judicial Council. The members of that council are the chief appellate judge of each of the 17 appellate districts and some judges from the Federal Court of Cassation. The council's presiding officer is a judge from the Supreme Federal Court. The council bears ultimate responsibility for all matters in the judicial branch. On several occasions in the early 2000s, it challenged the practices of Ministry of Interior police agencies. In 2006 the two-chamber Central Criminal Court of Iraq, established in 2003 by the Coalition Provisional Authority, retained authority to investigate and try crimes of national significance such as smuggling and insurgency. For military cases, civilian judges are named to a specially convened military court.

Administrative Divisions: Iraq has 18 governorates (provinces), which are divided into a total of 102 districts.

Provincial and Local Government: From Iraq's independence in 1932 until approval of the 2005 constitution, provincial and local governments were completely subordinate to the central government. The constitution of 2005 allots wide powers to the federal government but explicitly stipulates shared powers in customs, health, education, and environmental and natural resource policy and relegates all nonstipulated authority to the subnational jurisdictions. An article of the constitution still under discussion in mid-2006 provides for a new level of subnational jurisdiction, the region, which could include one or more governorates (provinces). Each region would elect its own government and have its own constitution. Governorates would have the option to remain independent of any region and to retain their own executive, legislative, and judicial institutions. As of mid-2006, Shiite and Kurdish leaders had endorsed the concept of regions as a basis of federalism, but no jurisdictional modifications had occurred. Governorates are subdivided into districts, which also are administered by elected councils. At the lowest level of subnational governance are municipalities and townships. In 2006 councils were in place in all 18 governorates, 90 districts, and 427 municipalities and townships. The governorate legislative councils each had 41 seats except for Baghdad's, which had 51.

In 1992 the Kurdish Iraqi Front organized elections in which the three Kurdish provinces of northern Iraq elected the autonomous Kurdistan National Assembly. According to the Transitional Administrative Law (TAL) and the constitution of 2005, the 111-member Kurdish Parliament elected in January 2005 has jurisdiction on all matters except foreign policy, diplomatic representation, security, defense, and fiscal matters including currency. Those matters are the responsibility of Iraq's national government. The seats of the Kurdish Parliament are divided between the two major Kurdish parties, with designated seats for the Assyrian Christian minority. Massoud Barzani was elected president of the Kurdistan Autonomous Region in 2005.

Judicial and Legal System: Under the regime of Saddam Hussein, the judicial system was fully controlled by the executive branch. One aim of the Transitional Administrative Law (TAL) was to restore an independent judiciary. However, chronically poor security conditions have prevented that system from functioning on a regular basis. In 2004 a British program began identifying and retraining Iraqi judges and legal personnel to replenish the court system. The legal system in place, pending comprehensive renovation under a permanent government, combines elements of Iraq's pre-Baathist laws and international law. In that system, which was influenced by French, Egyptian, and Ottoman law and is considered seriously outdated, judges rather than lawyers dominate court proceedings. Decisions are made by a three-judge panel; there are no juries. Since 2003 Iraq's court system has been moved from the Ministry of Justice to the jurisdiction of the Supreme Judicial Council, removing the influence of the executive branch that marked the Hussein regime.

The system is divided into civil and criminal courts and courts of personal status (for matters to be tried under Islamic law). Criminal courts are of two types, misdemeanor and felony. The hierarchy begins with courts of first instance, then district appeals courts (existing in 17 districts), courts of cassation, and the Federal Court of Cassation, which normally is the final appeal stage. Extraordinary cases go to the highest level, the Supreme Federal Court.

In an effort to curb violent crime, the interim government reinstated the death penalty in 2004 for crimes including drug trafficking and kidnapping. In 2005 Iraqi criminal courts sentenced several men to death for building terrorist bombs. On several occasions in the early 2000s, judges and lawyers suffered violence and intimidation. Reportedly, some 800 judges were active in 2006.

The interim government assigned an Iraq Special Tribunal for Crimes Against Humanity, including about 50 judges, to try top members of Saddam Hussein's regime, including Saddam Hussein himself, for war crimes as defined by the International Criminal Court. After the replacement of some judges caused substantial delays, the trial of Hussein began in October 2005 and continued intermittently through the summer of 2006. The composition, expertise, and scope of the special tribunal remained controversial in Iraq and among international authorities.

Electoral System: The minimum voting age is 18. Elections are supervised by the Independent Electoral Commission, a federal agency under the supervision of the Council of Representatives. Under the permanent government, the Supreme Federal Court has final approval authority for election results. Following approval of a national constitution in October 2005, new parliamentary elections chose a permanent Council of Representatives. Of the 275 seats filled, 230 were distributed in proportion to population among the 18 governorates (provinces). As the most populous, the Baghdad Governorate was allotted 59 seats. The remaining 45 seats were distributed as "compensation" to parties whose vote totals exceeded their proportional representation among the first 230 seats. The electoral system stipulates that at least one-quarter of National Assembly deputies must be women; the first permanent parliament had 69 women. All of Iraq's ethnic and religious communities also must be represented. The official turnout for the parliamentary elections of December 2005 was 79.6 percent, compared with 58 percent in the elections for the transitional parliament 11 months earlier. The disparity was partly the result of a substantial boycott by Sunnis of the first election.

Politics and Political Parties: Although Shia leader Ayatollah Sistani had opposed the formation of political organizations, he approved the formation of a Shia-dominated coalition, the United Iraqi Alliance, to contest the parliamentary elections of January 2005. In the early post–Saddam Hussein years, the two major formal Shia parties were the Supreme Council for the

Islamic Revolution (SCIRI) and Islamic Dawa (known as Dawa). SCIRI maintains close ties in Iran, commands a militia force of 10,000, and seeks a strong political role for the Islamic clergy. Since its return from exile in Iran in 2003, SCIRI has projected a more pluralistic image in a successful effort to broaden its support. It has supported the U.S. presence in Iraq and the 2005 parliamentary elections. Dawa began in 1958 as an Islamic revolutionary party, existed in exile during the Hussein regime, and emerged as an advocate of Islamic reform and modernization of religious institutions. In the parliamentary elections of January 2005, the United Iraqi Alliance gained 140 of the 275 seats contested, and Dawa leader Ibrahim al Jafari was named prime minister of the transitional government. In the parliamentary elections of December 2005, influential radical Shia leader Moqtada al Sadr brought his faction into the United Iraqi Alliance, which meanwhile lost the backing of Sistani and the participation of an important third party, the Iraqi National Congress. In those elections, the alliance lost 12 seats compared with January 2005. Of the alliance's constituent parties, in 2006 SCIRI held 36 seats in the Council of Representatives; the Sadr Party, 28; the Islamic Virtue Party, 15; and Dawa, 13. Nevertheless, Dawa leader Nouri al Maliki was a compromise appointment as prime minister of the first permanent government.

Iraq's Kurds are represented by two major parties, which since 2003 have cooperated in the government of the Kurdish Autonomous Region. Both parties have supported the U.S. presence in Iraq and played important roles in interim governments. The secular, nationalist Kurdistan Democratic Party (KDP) is the larger of the two parties and held one of two vice presidencies in the Interim Iraqi Government. Founded by the main Kurdish tribe, the Barzanis, the KDP has established good relations with the Turkish government. The Popular Union of Kurdistan, led by Jalal Talabani, also has a secular nationalist agenda and represents Kurds closest to the Iran border. In the parliamentary elections of January 2005, the Kurdish alliance of the two parties gained 75 seats, second to the United Iraqi Alliance. In the elections of December 2005, the alliance lost 22 seats but still held the second largest block in the Council of Representatives.

Several nonsectarian parties have played important roles in Iraqi politics since the fall of Saddam Hussein. The Iraqi National Congress (INC), led by Ahmed Chalabi, is a coalition with a large militia and strong ties in the southern Shia community, although Chalabi's influence in the government waned significantly after 2003. The INC, which advocates economic privatization and a secular government, held 13 seats in the transitional parliament as part of the United Iraqi Alliance. Iraqi National Accord (al Wilfaq) is led by Ayad Allawi, who was prime minister of the Interim Iraqi Government and remained an influential opposition figure in the permanent government. Despite Allawi's prominence and U.S. backing, the party fared poorly in the December 2005 elections. The Iraqi Communist Party (ICP) had its greatest influence in the 1960s, then substantially changed its agenda during the 1990s. Since 2003 the ICP has been represented in interim governments and maintains some support among secular Shias and Sunnis.

The largest official Sunni party is the Iraqi Islamic Party, whose leader Tariq al Hashimi was elected vice president in the first permanent government. That party is the foundation of the Sunni Iraqi Accord Front, which gained 44 seats in the parliamentary elections of December 2005. The Muslim Scholars' Association, formed in 2004, represents the senior Islamic scholars who set religious policy for the Sunni community. The association has strongly opposed the U.S.

presence in Iraq and successfully called for a boycott of the January 2005 parliamentary elections. Although the association also worked with Shia organizations for reconciliation of individual issues, on overall policy it diverged from the position of the Iraqi Accord Front, which participated actively in reconciliation talks in 2005 and 2006. In mid-2006, the kidnapping of a Sunni member of parliament incited a boycott of sessions by representatives of the front. The senior Sunni politician in Iraq, former foreign minister Adnan Pachachi, endorsed the new government and urged Sunni participation. Several smaller parties represent the Assyrian and Turkmen ethnic minorities.

Mass Media: After the end of full state control in 2003, a period of considerable growth occurred in Iraq's broadcast media. In 2005 about 80 radio stations and 25 television stations were broadcasting in Arabic, Kurdish, Turkmen, and Assyrian. The most popular television stations were the independent al Sharqiya and state-owned al Iraqiya. Arabic-language satellite broadcasts from neighboring countries were increasingly popular. The broadcast media, most of which were owned by political factions, presented both positive and negative positions on participation in the national elections of 2005. As of 2006, conditions did not make the operation of commercial media outlets profitable. Since the end of media oppression in 2003, newspapers in Iraq have presented a wide variety of views on critical issues. Nevertheless, in 2005 the Iraqi Association of Journalists reported some incidents of censorship by U.S. occupation forces, which also were accused of manipulating reports in nominally independent newspapers. The daily papers with the largest circulation, all published in Baghdad, are *al Mada*, *al Mutamar*, *al Sabah*, and *al Zaman* (also published in London). *Al Mutamar* is the official organ of the Iraqi National Congress, and *al Sabah* often reflects the positions of the government. An offshoot of *al Sabah,* called *al Sabah al Jadeed*, has taken a more independent position. *Al Mada* is a well-respected independent daily. The Iraqi News Agency is the main domestic news agency; major foreign news agencies with offices in Iraq are the Anadolu Ajansı of Turkey, the Associated Press of the United States, the Deutsche Presse-Agentur of Germany, the Informatsionnoye Telegrafnoye Agenstvo Rossii–Telegrafnoye Agenstvo Suverennykh Stran (ITAR—TASS) of the Russian Federation, Reuters of Britain, and Tsinhua of the People's Republic of China.

Foreign Relations: Because of the primary roles taken by the United States and Britain in deposing Saddam Hussein and establishing interim governments to replace his regime, Iraq's relationships with those countries, particularly the United States, are expected to remain paramount for the foreseeable future. Government and nongovernmental aid from the United States will continue as a crucial support in reconstruction. In 2006 formulation of more precise foreign policy priorities awaits the firm establishment of the permanent government. In the short term, Iraq's relations with Western and Far Eastern economic powers are determined by debt forgiveness and reconstruction assistance, which have come from many quarters. Relations with the United States were strained in mid-2006 when Iraq criticized Israeli attacks on Hezbollah forces in Lebanon.

Relations with Iraq's Sunni Arab neighbors have been conditioned by the degree of support for the 2003 regime change that empowered Iraq's Shia majority and by the need to curb the movement of insurgents from neighbors Jordan, Saudi Arabia, and Syria. Jordan's ambivalent role in the overthrow of Saddam Hussein cooled Iraq's normally close relations with that country. In 2005 relations with Jordan worsened when an ostensibly Jordanian suicide bomber killed 125 Iraqis. Traditional territorial disputes with Kuwait remained quiet in the early 2000s, and Iraq retained important commercial agreements with both Jordan and Kuwait. Since 2003, relations with neighboring Syria and Saudi Arabia have been harmed by what is seen as those countries' poor border security, which has allowed insurgents to move into and out of Iraq.

Iraq's relations with Iran, always complex, have depended on the approach taken by Iran's Shia government toward factional politics in Iraq. Since 2003 Iran's aims have been to prevent the resurrection of a strong, threatening Iraq while at the same time avoiding a collapse of Iraq into a civil war that might spread eastward. The optimal outcome for Iran would be establishment of a Shia-dominated government with at least some Islamic principles. As of mid-2006, Iran had not overtly used its extensive Shia connections within Iraq to destabilize governments, although that strategy remained available, and Iran has supported a Shia party, the Supreme Council for Islamic Revolution, in Iraqi politics. An important regional issue is water sharing with Syria and Turkey, who have restricted the flow of the Tigris and Euphrates into Iraq by building upstream dams. In 2006 resolution of that issue awaited policy decisions by the new permanent government in Iraq. In 2006 Iraq approved construction of an oil pipeline connecting neighbors Iran and Syria across Iraq's territory.

Membership in International Organizations: In 2006 Iraq was a member of the following international organizations: Arab Bank for Economic Development in Africa, Arab Fund for Economic and Social Development, Arab Monetary Fund, Council of Arab Economic Unity, Food and Agriculture Organization of the United Nations, Group of 77, International Atomic Energy Agency, International Criminal Police Organization (Interpol), International Development Association, International Federation of Red Cross and Red Crescent Societies, International Finance Corporation, International Fund for Agricultural Development, International Labour Organization, International Maritime Organization, International Monetary Fund, International Olympic Committee, International Standards Organization, International Telecommunication Union, Islamic Development Bank, League of Arab States, Organization of Arab Petroleum Exporting Countries, Organization of the Islamic Conference, Organization of the Petroleum Exporting Countries, United Nations, United Nations Committee on Trade and Development, United Nations Educational, Scientific and Cultural Organization, United Nations Industrial Development Organization, Universal Postal Union, World Customs Organization, World Federation of Trade Unions, World Health Organization, World Intellectual Property Organization, World Tourism Organisation, and World Trade Organization (observer status).

Major International Treaties: Among the multilateral treaties to which Iraq is a signatory are the Biological and Toxin Weapons Convention; Convention on the Prohibition of Military or Any Other Hostile Use of Environmental Modification Techniques (signed but not ratified); Geneva Conventions; Treaty on the Non-Proliferation of Nuclear Weapons; and United Nations Convention on the Law of the Sea.

NATIONAL SECURITY

Armed Forces Overview: In May 2003, the armed forces of Iraq were disbanded by the Coalition Provisional Authority (CPA) that took control after Saddam Hussein was toppled. This process included the destruction of large amounts of military equipment. With training from forces and agencies of the United States, Britain, and other members of the CPA, new security forces underwent organization and training in the early 2000s. Occupation forces screened and organized former military and police personnel as the near-term basis for security forces, following reversal of a 2003 decision to disband all Iraqi forces. The predominance of Shias and Kurds in the new army and national guard has caused resentment in the Sunni population. Despite high unemployment, terrorist acts against the Iraqi military and police have depressed recruitment. In March 2005, the minister of interior predicted that Iraq's security forces would be fully staffed and competent in 18 months. As of mid-2006, some 254,000 security troops had been trained; the goal was to train 325,000 by the end of 2006. However, the reliability of those forces remained dubious, according to Western sources.

Foreign Military Relations: Beginning in 2003, the coalition forces in Iraq, particularly U.S. and British, performed the bulk of security operations and provided all military training for Iraqi units; the United States was the source of Iraq's military budget. Notably lacking in the coalition were France, Germany, and Russia, which opposed the 2003 military action against Saddam Hussein and provided little support in the two years that followed. Of 21 countries with troops in Iraq in mid-2006, three besides the United States (Britain, South Korea, and Italy) had more than 1,000 troops; Italy announced plans for full withdrawal of its 2,900 troops by the end of 2006. Ukraine, which had had 1,650 troops in Iraq, completed its withdrawal in 2005; Poland, which had 900 troops remaining in 2006, postponed full withdrawal in midyear.

External Threat: In 2005 and 2006, unknown numbers of insurgents crossed the borders of Iran, Jordan, Saudi Arabia, and Syria in order to mount terrorist attacks inside the country. This situation accelerated the training of border police and the construction of new border installations. Three training facilities were established in 2005, with the aim of preparing 11,000 border troops. Technology at existing points of entry was to be upgraded in 2006. Iraq was not the target of conventional attack from any outside force.

Defense Budget: The interim government of Iraq budgeted US$2 billion for military expenditures in 2004.

Major Military Units: The ground forces will account for the majority of the personnel envisioned in the Iraqi Armed Forces. The New Iraqi Army, which had about 100,000 troops in 2006, including National Guard forces, will be purely defensive and represent all the major factions in Iraq's population. The initial organizational structure includes light infantry brigades (possibly one division), rapid intervention forces, and special forces. The light infantry units will not have the firepower or logistical capability to conduct independent counterinsurgency operations.

Plans call for a small naval force. In 2005 an estimated 700 naval personnel were active. In 2003 British Royal Navy units began training a small Iraqi Riverine Patrol Service, which eventually is to have 400 personnel and 22 patrol boats to regulate trafficking and illegal entry into the country via the Shatt al Arab. In 2005 Iraq deployed a Coastal Defense Force trained by the British Royal Navy and stationed at Umm Qasr with 10 patrol boats for use in the northern Persian Gulf.

Plans call for a small air force whose main function will be reconnaissance of borders and potential targets of terrorist attack. In 2005 three squadrons, totaling about 200 personnel, performed domestic transport and reconnaissance operations.

Major Military Equipment: Iraqi equipment remaining intact after the war of 2003 and suitable for future use is to be absorbed into the new armed forces. The nature and numbers of that equipment are not known. In 2004 the air force had two Seeker reconnaissance aircraft; plans call for purchasing eight more.

Military Service: In 2006 Iraq had no conscription system, although a draft system could be established by the permanent government. Recruitment centers were located in Arbil, Baghdad, Basra, and Mosul.

Paramilitary Forces: The number of personnel in Iraq's paramilitary organizations has fluctuated frequently, decreasing when violence against such units has intensified. In 2006 the Ministry of Interior security organizations, aside from the police, had an estimated 32,900 active personnel divided into four main functions: border enforcement, civil intervention, emergency response, and dignitary protection. The border enforcement personnel, 21,600 strong in 2006, included border police, a Bureau of Civil Customs Inspection, and a Bureau of Immigration Inspection. Plans called for 32,000 border personnel and 254 border installations. The Iraqi National Guard, formerly called the Iraqi Civil Defense Corps, had about 40,000 active personnel in 2005, when it was absorbed nominally into the regular ground forces. Nevertheless, in 2006 National Guard units still reportedly were conducting independent missions and were linked with antigovernment militia activity. The Facilities Protection Service (FPS), staffed mainly by former military and security personnel, was nominally under the Ministry of Interior but by 2005 had become an independent for-hire force, paid by private security companies to protect oil industry and government installations. In response to reports linking the FPS with death squad activities, the Ministry of Interior attempted in 2006 to limit the operations of the FPS, whose size reportedly had grown to 145,000.

Foreign Military Forces: In mid-2006, an estimated 127,000 U.S. troops and 19,000 non-U.S. coalition troops from 20 countries were in Iraq. Another 17 countries had fully withdrawn military personnel from Iraq by mid-2006 after participating in the occupation. An additional 20,000 private military contractors were in place.

Police: During the regime of Saddam Hussein, Iraq's law enforcement system was marked by corruption and inhumane practices. After the previous police force was completely disbanded, in 2003 a new Iraqi Police Service was established to act as a municipal law enforcement agency under the authority of the Ministry of Interior. The Police Service does not conduct investigative operations, but it has been assigned to support some operations of coalition military forces. In 2006 a nominal total of 135,000 police personnel had undergone training, but the training level and reliability of this force were in question. The number of police personnel actually on duty has fluctuated significantly; in 2004 the number dropped from 85,000 to 44,000 in response to attacks on police units. Officially, some 28 police battalions were on duty in 2006. Plans call for a highway patrol element to be added in the future.

The police have been accused of politically motivated attacks on non-Shia Iraqis. Two Shia militia groups, the Badr Organization (the armed wing of the Supreme Council for the Islamic Revolution (SCIRI) party) and the Army of the Mahdi, have substantially infiltrated police forces in some regions. Police operations in the Kurdish Autonomous Region, where the Ministry of Interior officially lacks jurisdiction, are controlled by Kurdish militias. From the beginning of the occupation in 2003, the new Iraqi police force has been the target of attacks, kidnappings, and murders. The government estimated that 280 police were killed between 2003 and January 2006.

Experts consider reform of the police system a long and difficult process. In 2004 starting pay for police personnel was US$60 per month plus a hazardous duty allowance of an additional US$87 per month. As under the Hussein regime, police corruption, extortion, and theft have continued to be problematic. In the elections of 2005, the National Guard and police provided polling place security that monitors characterized as adequate, under threats of large-scale insurgent disruption.

The Iraqi National Intelligence Service (INIS) was established in 2004 in cooperation with the U.S. Central Intelligence Agency (CIA) to gather information on groups threatening national security. The president is to appoint the director of the INIS, which is to serve as an information agency for the Council of Ministers and have no law enforcement authority.

Internal Threat: In 2005 estimates of the number of insurgents in Iraq varied widely from 30,000 to 200,000. According to one 2005 report, 90 percent of the 30,000 insurgents present were Iraqis, and most foreign insurgents came from Algeria, Sudan, Syria, and Yemen. Insurgent forces, concentrated in Sunni-dominated central Iraq, were organized by surviving leaders of the Baathist establishment. An organization central to this threat is Tanzim Qaidat al Jihad fi Bilad al Rafidayn (TQJBR), which was led by the Jordanian extremist Abu Musab al Zarqawi until his death in May 2006. TQJBR's objectives are to expel the multinational coalition forces from Iraq and establish a state under Islamic law, and to this end it has allied itself with the global anti-Western jihad of al Qaeda. The level of violence in Iraq increased in the months following Zarqawi's death.

Many independent militia groups also are believed responsible for attacks. Following the formation of a permanent government, sectarian violence between Shia and Sunni militias escalated sharply in the spring and summer of 2006, increasing fears of a full-scale civil war. The United Nations estimated that such violence killed more than 4,300 civilians in the first half of 2006. In 2006 the Shia leader Moqtada al Sadr emerged as the strongest militia leader. Headquartered in An Najaf, al Sadr's militia, the Mahdi Army, had tens of thousands of fighters in mid-2006. Its power was magnified by the dominant position in the parliament of al Sadr's political party, the United Iraqi Alliance.

In the absence of effective security, conventional crime also increased significantly beginning in 2003. Kidnapping for ransom and the trafficking of women and workers continued to increase in 2005 and 2006. The trafficking activity took advantage of Iraq's loose border controls.

Terrorism: Since the toppling of Saddam Hussein in May 2003, coalition military forces, Iraqis involved with reconstruction, and the general public have been endangered by a variety of bombings, kidnappings, and executions conducted by insurgent forces believed to be primarily Sunni and of both domestic and foreign origin. Their particular targets have been Iraqi police and military personnel and trainees, but in 2006 civilians increasingly were targeted. Many terrorist acts have been unattributed, and many apparently independent militias are known to have participated in them.

Human Rights: In the early post–Saddam Hussein era, some forms of human rights abuses continued to exist in Iraq, aside from those implicit in a society racked by terrorist acts. A national state of emergency, first declared in 2004 and ongoing in 2006, authorized the federal government to restrict public gatherings, monitor communications, and detain suspects in ways conflicting with normal human rights protections. The Iraqi Corrections Service, which continued to run the official prison system, met most international prison standards in 2005 after making significant improvement. Nevertheless, reports still cited instances of prisoner abuse and torture, overcrowding, and substandard medical care. Conditions in unofficial detention centers known to exist were unverified. The Iraqi National Guard, responsible for domestic security, was charged with abuse of detainees and the coercion of confessions, as were local police and security agencies of the Ministry of Interior. Specialized agencies such as the National Intelligence Service were charged with violating pretrial procedures. In a society whose mores reportedly became more conservative in the early 2000s, women's rights suffered, and crimes against women increased. A Ministry of State for Women's Affairs existed but remained unfunded in 2005.

Under the Transitional Administrative Law and in the first year of the 2005 constitution, the judicial system generally has functioned fairly, given its inherent limitations. Backlogs in the system have led to long pretrial detention, and in some cases detainees have not been notified of their status. Some illegal detentions were documented. The government has not impeded the work of foreign journalists, although several have been kidnapped or murdered, and access to especially dangerous locations has been restricted.